C000121124

THIS BOOK BELONGS TO:

Printed in Great Britain
by Amazon

20881317R00059